JOHNNY McKEE
and the
BIG FLOOD

By IRMENGARDE EBERLE

Illustrated by SAM SAVITT

Originally published in 1960
Cover design by Tina DeKam
© 2021 Jenny Phillips
goodandbeautiful.com

Table of Contents

🌿 1 🌿

THE VISIT

WHEN Johnny McKee and his family were about a half-mile from the Everses' truck farm, Johnny began to get excited. He had been sitting in the back of the car, and now he began to move around. He knelt on the seat cushion to look out the back window. He slid from side to side, and sometimes he stood up.

"Hey, quiet down, Johnny," his father called out.

"You're blocking the rear window, Johnny," his mother said. She was sitting in front with Dad.

Johnny sat down and kept still for a while. But it was hard because he wanted to see all the familiar

1

sights. He wished he could look in every direction at once.

He was going to have a fine time at the Everses' today. There were the two children to play with—Emily, a little younger than he, and four-year-old Bill. And there was their dog, Mac, who was smooth haired and brown and white and liked to play. Johnny loved Mac almost as much as he did his own yellow cat, Tim, back home.

Johnny liked all animals. And of all the kinds he knew, he liked horses best—even better than cats and dogs, maybe. It was too bad the Everses didn't have a horse. Johnny could not have one himself because he and his parents lived in Warren City, and there was no place for a stable.

Johnny thought of the horse on the Rolfs' dairy farm, not far from the Everses' place. He fingered the two lumps of sugar he had put in his pocket and looked about him. The Rolfs' farm must be near now. But down here in the valley, the trees and the curve of the hill cut off the sight of the house.

"Mother, Dad," he asked, "can I go over to the Rolfs' and see their horse sometime today?"

"Why not?" his father said.

His mother said, "Yes, it's all right for you to go if the Evers children don't mind. Just don't stay too long."

An idea began to grow in Johnny's head. He was going to ask the Rolfs something. He smiled to himself.

The day sparkled. It was a Saturday morning in the spring, about a month before school was out. The weather was mild and bright. The trees were lightly green. Wildflowers bloomed in the meadows and along the roadsides. Birds sang, and now and then a rabbit scampered off into the fields.

The McKees were traveling along the edge of curving Mill River. They came to a bridge, and their car rumbled loudly on its wood and steel. As they crossed it onto a side road, Johnny looked out over the bridge railing and saw the rippling water of the river. The car hurried on, out of the valley and into a narrow country lane, the Everses' own farm road, running between neat fields in which green young shoots were beginning to show.

Johnny put on his broad-brimmed Western hat and reached for the box of candy he and his parents had brought for their friends. He wriggled again.

His mother laughed, feeling the excitement too. "I'll be glad to see the Everses," she said. "It's been four months since we've seen them. That's a long while for two people who are as old friends as Nora Evers and I are. Why, we've known each other since we were children."

The car swung into the driveway at last and stopped before the low white house. On the front lawn Emily and Bill, and Mac their dog, stood waiting. The sight of them made Johnny feel good.

Emily and Bill shouted, "They're here!" and "Here they are!" and "Hi, Johnny! Hi, Aunt Jean and Uncle Dan!"

They came running to the car as Johnny and his parents climbed out. Mac barked.

The grown-up Everses, Aunt Nora and Uncle Howard, hearing the shouting and noise, came out of the house and welcomed their friends.

As he recognized the guests, Mac stopped barking and let Johnny pet him. Johnny was always surprised that the dog remembered him so well from his short visits many months apart.

He gave the box of candy to Emily and Bill.

"Oh, thanks," Emily cried. "Candy!"

Bill took it and ran to show it to his mother and father.

"Look what Johnny gave us!" he cried.

Mrs. Evers said, "Lovely. Well, that's certainly very nice of the McKees." She took the box from Bill, saying, "You can all have some of it after lunch."

"OK," Bill said to his mother, and then to the others, "Let's play." He took Johnny's hand and pulled him. "Come."

"OK," said Johnny.

"You've got your Western hat on, Johnny," Emily noticed.

The children played on the lawn for only a few minutes before Mrs. Evers called them in for lunch.

Lunch was good. But as soon as the children had finished, they were outdoors again, and now each had a piece of candy. Mac had been waiting by the front door for them. He ran around them and waggled all over. The children brought him bits of fried chicken and a piece of cake. He gulped them quickly. Then Johnny romped with him on the lawn and threw sticks for the dog to retrieve. Johnny rolled over in the grass, and Mac pranced around him, barking. At last Johnny sat up, and Mac lay down beside him.

Johnny thought of the Rolfs' horse and longed for him.

Emily had been watching and laughing at Mac. Now she said, "Let's go on a journey."

Johnny put on his Western hat again, and Bill ran and brought his out. Emily got the old, red pocketbook that had been her mother's until it became so worn. Each of them took one more piece of candy, and they set out.

The first stop was the tool house. The lawn mower stood there, and Johnny fiddled with it for a while.

Next the children went to look at the tent that Bill and Emily used as a playhouse. After that they climbed a tree.

Then Johnny said, "Let's go to the brook and look for rabbits and squirrels and chipmunks in the woods down there."

"Let's," said Emily.

"Sure," said Bill.

Emily thought they might even see a raccoon. Johnny knew that raccoons were night-prowling animals and only rarely came out of their hiding places in the daytime. He had read about them in one of his books. Still, he certainly wanted to look for one.

They all started out along a narrow dirt road. Then the children remembered about Mac. Certainly no wild animals would come out to play or to drink at the brook if he was there. The children would have to leave him behind. Emily and Johnny caught him by his collar and pulled him toward the house. The dog struggled to get loose. Johnny felt sorry for him, and so did Emily.

"We'll be right back," Johnny said.

"Poor Mac. We won't leave you for long," said Emily.

When they reached the house, Bill ran in and asked his parents to keep the dog indoors for a while. They agreed, and the children brought Mac in and latched the screen doors so that he couldn't push them open.

Johnny hated to leave Mac. He and Emily and Bill ran off quickly so that they wouldn't hear him whine and beg inside the back door.

They skirted a long narrow field that had been newly plowed, walked across a small patch of wild meadow, and were among the trees and bushes that made a little wood. There they followed a dim path that Emily and Bill had made.

Suddenly Emily warned Johnny to be quiet and pointed to the branch of a young tree. There, hidden among the leaves and branches, they could just barely see a mother bird on her nest. Only her head was in view. Her bright eyes were alert, watchful. The children tiptoed by.

"Boy, this is a swell place," Johnny said when they were far enough away not to disturb the bird.

They ran down a stony slope and came to a little stream of clear water that trickled between mossy rocks. Jumping across it, they went into the brush beyond. Two squirrels rushed up a tree. Another animal darted away among the green brush where some of last autumn's dry leaves still lay. It made a rustling sound, but the children could not see the creature.

They spread out through the little wood, hunting for a raccoon or maybe an opossum. Johnny and Bill went one way and Emily another. But Bill was small and could barely get through the brush in places. He found it very hard to keep up with Johnny, and the twigs scratched his face and knocked his hat off. He yelled, and Johnny went to him and took him piggyback.

But the children did not find any raccoons or opossums—only a rabbit or two and some more squirrels. After a while they came together again. Standing on a big flat rock above the brook, they threw stones into the water and watched them splash.

After a while Johnny again thought about the dairy farm across the river. He would certainly like to see the herd of cows and the calves and the chickens. And, of course, most of all he wanted to see the horse. He told Emily and Bill about it and explained that his parents had said he could go to the Rolfs'.

"Want to come with me?" he asked.

"Oh, we can't," Emily said.

"We can't ever go across the bridge without Mommy and Daddy," Bill told him. "We promised."

Johnny was disappointed. "Honest?"

Emily nodded. "You don't really want to go there, do you, Johnny?" she asked. "I wish you wouldn't."

But Johnny did want to go, very much. "Please let me," he said. "I won't stay long—only about fifteen minutes or so. It's just so I can see the horse. I want to give him some sugar lumps."

Emily and Bill gave in. "OK, Bill and I will go play with poor old Mac," Emily said, "so he won't have to stay indoors anymore."

"OK," said Johnny. "Honestly, I won't stay away long."

The three children had come up out of the woods and were at the field road. There they parted.

Emily and Bill turned toward home. Johnny went westward toward Mill River. He turned and waved before he went down the slope to the river bottom; then he was among tall trees.

In another minute he came to the bridge he had recently crossed in the family car. On the other side lay the main road. He crossed it and went up the slope beyond, going through a meadow, brightly green with grass and weeds. Now he could see the Rolfs' house, barn, and silo at the top of the long low hill. He hurried his steps. Mr. Rolf was at work with his plow in a field to the north. In the kitchen garden, near the house, Mrs. Rolf was weeding. Chickens cackled. Johnny went up the rise beyond the house and saw the cattle grazing in the meadow. There was the horse, too, not far from the upper fence. The Rolfs' two gray cats were walking daintily over the lawn, and Johnny called to them. But they went on, bound on business of their own.

Johnny walked over to the vegetable garden. Mrs. Rolf's tomato plants were already up, and other things were growing, too. All of them looked fine and sturdy.

"Hello, Mrs. Rolf," he said.

"Hello, young fellow," she answered, looking up at him. "Aren't you the son of those friends of Howard Evers?"

"Yes, I'm Johnny McKee." He was glad she remembered him. "When will those plants have tomatoes?" he asked her after a moment.

"Well before midsummer," she said, "because they were planted early. Don't they look fine? They're my special pride."

Johnny agreed. Then he asked, "Do you mind if I go and pet your horse?"

"Not at all," said Mrs. Rolf. "Go right along. He's in the pasture with the cows, down there. But the cows are a little farther off. They won't bother you."

Johnny wasn't afraid of the cows. But he had another question in mind. "Can I ride him?" he asked.

"Why, yes," Mrs. Rolf told him. She set the hoe against the side of the open gate to the garden and leaned on a post. "Red Boy will be glad to take you on his back," she said. "He used to belong to our son, who's grown up now. He's married and lives away off in Pennsylvania. Now the horse has no

13

one to ride him. And what with all the farm machinery we have nowadays, we don't even use him for farm work much. He'll be glad of your company."

Johnny's face glowed with pleasure as she spoke. "Gosh, thanks," he said, and started to go.

She called after him. "There's a bridle in the barn, way over this side." She gestured with her hands. "Near where his stall is. The saddle is too heavy for you to put on alone. You can ride bareback, though. He's very gentle."

Of course he could ride bareback, Johnny said, and thanked her again. Boy, this was wonderful!

"Can you put a bridle on a horse?" Mrs. Rolf asked.

"Sure I can," Johnny said. He had done it at the riding farm that used to be near Warren City. His parents sometimes had taken him to ride there. He hurried to get the bridle, found it, and took it outside. The gate to the pasture was fastened with a wire loop over a post. He lifted the wire and swung the gate open.

"Hi, Red Boy!" he called out, and walked across the grassy meadow.

The horse lifted his head. He did not know the boy, but he was not afraid. Johnny took the two sugar lumps from his pocket and held them out on the flat palm of his hand. The horse ate them, leaving Johnny's hand damp. Johnny grinned, wiped his hand on his pants, then patted Red Boy and stroked his nose. The horse nuzzled his shoulder.

Johnny put the bit in the horse's mouth. He took it easily. Then Johnny slipped the strap over the horse's head and fastened the buckle. But without a saddle and stirrups, Johnny couldn't get on Red Boy. He led him up the slope to the fence. There, using the wire fence and the gatepost as a ladder, he climbed onto Red Boy's broad back. Then he rode through the gate to the farm road. Mr. Rolf, in the field away off toward the north, saw him and hallooed, and Johnny shouted back and waved. Mrs. Rolf smiled and went on with her weeding.

Johnny felt glorious riding on the horse. It seemed to him that the birds were singing more loudly than before. There was nothing so fine in all the world as a horse. And this was the best of them

Johnny climbed onto Red Boy's back

all, a horse that acted as though Johnny had been his friend all his life.

Here in the open, on the broad slope, he could see more of the cows. There were about thirty of them, and some were coming nearer the house. The calves were in their separate smaller pasture. Farther off he could see the Mill River glinting in the sun. With his eyes he could follow its course by its fringe of trees and occasional patches of thick woodland. It made a great horseshoe curve around the broad, low hill on which the Rolfs' place stood.

He did not ride far. Remembering his promise to Emily and Bill to be back soon, he halted the horse within a few minutes and turned him back. After he had put Red Boy in the pasture again, he planned to take just a quick look at the Rolfs' chickens and maybe pet some of the calves.

Johnny and Red Boy were coming slowly toward the Rolfs' driveway when Johnny heard Mrs. Rolf's shout.

"The cows! The cows!"

Her voice sounded frantic. Johnny looked toward the pasture. A few of the cows were at the upper part of the land. But suddenly Johnny saw that one was coming through the gate he had left open, and others were already on the lawn, nibbling grass and trampling on a newly planted flower border. And two of them had found the open gate to Mrs. Rolf's kitchen garden. They had come into it while she was working, and she had not noticed.

"Out! Out!" she shouted desperately, waving her hoe at them. "They're ruining my garden—my tomatoes, my flower bed!"

Johnny slid from the horse, horrified at what was happening. He ran to the cows on the lawn and tried to chase them back. Mrs. Rolf screamed at him as well as at the cows all around her.

The cows dodged and shook their heads, not knowing what was wanted of them. They trotted around in confusion, and their hard hoofs crushed the new young tomato plants and the flower border still more.

It was terrible. Johnny and Mrs. Rolf were helpless. Mrs. Rolf shouted for Mr. Rolf. He heard and came running. The big, part-collie farm dog, who had been in the far-off field with him, came bounding along.

In a few minutes these two had driven the cows back into the pasture. While that was going on, Johnny caught the horse by his bridle and led him back toward the pasture too. Mr. Rolf met Johnny at the gate and took the horse from him. As he slipped the bridle off and hung it over his arm, he gave Johnny an angry glance but said nothing. He fastened the gate firmly and walked off to the barn with the bridle.

Johnny, back in the yard, looked at the awful ruin his carelessness had caused. Mrs. Rolf was kneeling by the broken tomato plants, trying to see if she could save any of them.

Johnny felt awful. "I'm sorry," he said. "I'm sorry, Mrs. Rolf. I never thought about the gate."

"Sorry?" she said furiously. "You're sorry—and look at this! No amount of being sorry will bring my garden back to the way it was."

He knew that was so. "Can I help try to fix it?" he asked in a low voice.

Johnny started away, feeling unhappy

"No," she said.

He stood there a while longer, wanting to do something helpful. At last he started away, his head hung down in unhappiness and regret.

Mrs. Rolf did not say good-bye to him, and he did not say good-bye, either. He walked along slowly, scuffing his feet. The big dog who was so good at herding cows trotted along with him a short way, then swerved off to the left to chase a rabbit.

When Johnny got to the Everses', Emily and Bill

were indoors, watching a television show. Mac was stretched out on the floor, asleep. He got up and wagged his tail, and Johnny patted his head.

"You were gone an awful long time," Emily said, hardly looking at him. She sounded a little cross.

"I was visiting the Rolfs' horse," Johnny said. "I like him." His voice was sad.

Emily looked at him again, more carefully. "What's the matter?" she asked.

He would not say. He felt too gloomy. Should he tell his parents? He decided against it. He had to think the whole thing out alone first. When he knew what he could do to make up to the Rolfs for what had happened, then he would tell his father and mother. He sat down on the floor in front of the television set with the other two children and drew Mac to him. But he could not pay attention to what was happening on the screen. He kept seeing the unhappy Rolfs and the gentle horse, Red Boy. Johnny almost groaned aloud. He had spoiled everything for himself as well as for the Rolfs.

21

They would never again let him ride Red Boy, and probably they would not want him to come to their place anymore. He wouldn't even be able to pet Red Boy.

The afternoon dragged on. After a while Johnny and Emily and Bill played outdoors again. But Johnny's heart wasn't in their games. He was almost glad when evening came and it was time to go home.

🌿 2 🌿

JOHNNY HAS A SECRET

Back in Warren City Johnny began to plan in secret. He would find a way, all alone, to make up to the Rolfs for the harm he had done. Meanwhile, he would tell no one of his trouble, no one at all, he decided.

His mother and father noticed that he seemed worried.

"What's troubling you?" his mother asked.

"Get into a quarrel with the Evers kids?" his father said.

Johnny shook his head. He couldn't tell them about the Rolfs' garden yet.

On Monday morning Johnny had to go to school. But his thoughts were still on the Rolfs and their horse. He was too troubled to pay much attention in class. The children noticed it, and so did his teacher.

"What's the matter?" Miss Comac asked him during reading period.

"Oh, nothing," Johnny said.

"Why not tell me and get it off your mind?" Miss Comac asked.

But he couldn't. He tried to pay attention, but in a minute he was thinking of his problem again. He could buy seeds for the Rolfs of course, he told himself, so that they could plant a new garden. But what a lot of work for them. And their garden would be very late. They wouldn't thank him much for that. Then he thought of how beautiful Red Boy was. How Johnny would like to rub him down and brush him till he shone like a policeman's horse.

At recess most of the girls headed toward the slides and swings. The boys made for the corner of

24

the big grounds where they could pitch and catch. Johnny's best friend, Bart Cole, walked close beside him.

"What's eating you?" he asked Johnny.

"Nothing," Johnny said again.

Bart shook his head. "We promised not to have any secrets from each other," he said.

That was true. In a rush Johnny told him. Bart was troubled. What had happened was a terrible thing.

"What are you going to do?" he asked, his eyes big with worry.

"I don't know yet," Johnny said. "Maybe I could buy baskets full of tomatoes and flowers this summer and send them to the Rolfs."

"Maybe," said Bart, "but I wish that you could think of something better."

"So do I," said Johnny.

They walked away from each other, and Johnny threw his ball for Bart to catch.

Walking home that afternoon, Johnny and Bart

again talked about Johnny's problem. How could he get to be friends with the Rolfs and their horse and cows again? They stopped to join up with Bart's beagle and to pet and talk to dogs and cats along the way. Ted and Ginger, two of their classmates, came and walked with them, and Johnny and Bart stopped making plans so that they would not give their secret away.

Several blocks from the two-story apartment house where Johnny lived there were some small new houses with lawns. And there was one large, old, white house set in the midst of spacious grounds. Out in back Mrs. Halloran, who lived there, was planting something.

Johnny and Bart saw this and, giving each other a secret look, went quickly to see what was going on. Ginger came along too, although the boys wished she hadn't, because of their secret.

Mrs. Halloran was sitting on the ground beside a newly dug garden patch. She had a trowel in her hand, and beside her in the grass stood flat boxes of very young plants—plants with the soil still around their roots. As the children talked with her, she took the plants one at a time and set them into the earth of her garden. This was interesting. She was making a garden out of ready-made plants.

Johnny asked her about them and found that each box was called a "flat" and held a dozen plants. Some held one kind of flower, some another.

"Where did you buy them?" Johnny asked.

"At Murch's Garden Store," she told him. "They have lots of them for sale."

"Honest?" Johnny was delighted.

"What do you want to know that for, Johnny?" Ginger asked. "You aren't going to plant a garden, are you?" She laughed. "You can't. You live in an apartment. You don't have any yard."

Bart answered for Johnny, "No, he's not going to plant a garden. He's just got to find out about something."

Johnny went on talking to Mrs. Halloran. "How much do those flats cost?"

"About two dollars each for these sets of flower plants," Mrs. Halloran told him.

That was a lot of money.

"Does Murch's have tomato plants, too?" Johnny asked.

"Oh, yes," Mrs. Halloran answered. "And they're quite a lot cheaper."

Johnny smiled. That was good. The tomato plants were more important. He remembered how Mrs. Rolf had said, "They're my special pride."

Again Ginger asked, "Why do you want to know about flats, Johnny?"

"Wait a minute, Ginger," Johnny said. He turned to Mrs. Halloran and thanked her for all she had told him. "I always did want to know about flats," he said. Then he and his friends started on their way.

"Now tell me, Johnny," Ginger said when they were back on the sidewalk in front of the house, "why do you want to know about flats?"

"I wish you hadn't come along," Johnny said, "because I don't really want to tell you, or anyone. Bart and I, we're the only ones who know. But now I guess we'll have to let you in on the secret. But don't you tell anyone."

"OK," said Ginger earnestly.

Johnny told her the story of the Rolfs, with Bart helping out.

Ginger was excited over the terrible story. "Oh, how can you ever make up for what the cows did?" she asked. "It seems hopeless."

Johnny was smiling. "Can't you see?" he asked. "I'm going to take them some ready-made young plants like Mrs. Halloran has. They'll be just about the size of the flower and tomato plants that got ruined."

"Oh." Ginger was suddenly all smiles. "That's a wonderful idea. You'll just take the plants out there and put them in her garden, and it will be almost exactly like it was before."

Johnny said, "Yes."

29

"That's it," said Bart.

"Maybe then I can walk around their farm again sometimes and be with Red Boy and the dog and cats and cows and calves and chickens till they know me really well," Johnny said.

He thought of his little bank with the slot in it which stood on his chest of drawers at home. It had no money in it at all. He had spent too much lately.

He said, "I'm going to need at least six or seven dollars to buy those plants for the Rolfs, I think. And I have to earn it fast."

"We'll help you if we can," Bart said. "We'll tell you if we get any good ideas."

"OK. Thanks," Johnny said. "And next time I go out to Uncle Howard and Aunt Nora Evers', I'll try to get a picture of the horse to show you."

They had reached Johnny's building, and now they parted. Johnny raced up the single flight of stairs to his family's apartment. There he said hello to his mother, picked up his cat, Tim, and went to get a chocolate and vanilla ice cream stick from the deep freeze.

"Mom, I want to earn some money. Do you have any work I could do?" he asked.

"I can't think of anything now, but I'll try to find some odd jobs for you," his mother said.

Johnny took the cat and went into his room to think. After a while he decided to go into a small part of the plumbing repair business. He had often helped his father put a new washer in a faucet. Around this neighborhood there must be lots of faucets that needed new washers. Last year, too, he had put the old Christmas tree lights in order by himself. Maybe he could do some electrical work.

After dinner he cut some white paper to the size of business cards, while his cat, Tim, rolled a pencil around on the desk with his soft paw. Then Johnny set up some type in his type box and printed a dozen cards. Here is what Johnny wrote:

JOHN McKEE

Plumbing Repairs

Christmas Tree Lights Fixed

233 PRESTON STREET, WARREN CITY

TELEPHONE WO 5-4572

Of course it was spring now, and he wouldn't get any Christmas tree work to do. But he put that line in because it showed his experience.

He took the cards to school with him the next day and showed one to Bart.

"They're my business cards," he told him.

"It's a neat idea to do plumbing repairs," Bart said. "And those cards are fine. I wish I'd had an idea like that, and I wish I had a printing outfit."

Later Johnny found Ginger with some other girls and called her away so that he could show her the cards. She admired them.

"Would you print twelve cards for me with my name on them?" she asked. "I'll give you a dime for that."

Of course he would. Here was another way he

could earn money. He and Ginger asked several children on the school grounds if they would like printed name cards. Some of them wanted cards, but no one would pay as much for them as Ginger. Johnny could see that this plan would bring in only pennies.

After school Bart went with Johnny while he left his cards at several houses along the way home. When he had given all of them away, he and Bart checked in with their mothers, then went to play ball.

Later, on his way home, Johnny thought about the horse, Red Boy, whom he might never again pet or ride. It made him sad.

But then he began to think about Mac, the Everses' dog, and about the wild animals that were living so secretly in the woods all around the farm. He stopped at the nearby library, took down a book about animals, and read about foxes and raccoons and opossums. By the time he got home, he felt better.

After dinner that night he printed twelve cards for Ginger and six for Bart, who was going to pay a nickel for them.

Several days went by but he did not receive any calls to put washers in faucets. He decided to go in person and ask for work. One man said he did all his small repairs himself. A woman reminded Johnny that one had to be a licensed plumber to do such work.

"I'll call you if I can think of some way you can help me," another neighbor said.

All this was getting him nowhere, Johnny decided. He must think up other ideas. He went to a nearby flower shop.

"Do you need a delivery boy?" he asked.

But the shop already had one. He walked on and was wondering what to try next when he passed the supermarket. Outside, Don Williams and some other boys about his own age were asking people to let them carry heavy packages.

"That's worth trying," he said to himself.

34

A neighbor from his own street came out of the market with two huge brown-paper bags full of groceries.

"Can I carry your bags for you for a quarter?" he asked eagerly.

"I'm only going a few steps to my car," the lady said.

"I'll take them for fifteen cents," Johnny offered.

"Fine," said the lady. "Here, you take one package and I'll keep the other. That way it won't be too much for either of us."

When he came back from this job, he tried another lady, and another. But they wanted to carry their own packages.

It was time to go home, and he felt good as he walked down the street. Here was a way to earn extra money.

At home he told his mother about the supermarket.

"May I go there every afternoon?" he asked.

"Why, yes, Johnny, I should think that would be

all right. But remember, carry packages only to people's cars or to their house doors," his mother said.

After that he went to the supermarket several times a week. Sometimes Bart came with him and earned extra money too. It was fun counting their nickels and dimes, and sometimes a quarter, afterward. In two weeks Johnny earned two dollars and forty-five cents. In addition, he had the money he saved from his allowance.

Sometimes he put all his allowance in the bank, except enough for a strawberry ice cream soda. He didn't really need more than one soda a week, he decided, because he could eat ice cream sticks from the deep freeze at home on other days. But he liked to go to the drugstore now and then. It was fun to order over the counter and to talk to the other boys and girls who were having soda or ice cream.

Coming home from his supermarket work one evening, he found his father already home from the office. He was sitting in the living room, reading his newspaper. His father's shoes, Johnny noticed, were a little dusty.

He went to him and said, "Hi, Dad. Can I shine your shoes for you? And will you pay me as much as you pay Sam your shoeshine man?"

"Well, I don't know," Mr. McKee said. "Sam's an expert at it. But I'll pay you, say—"

"Fifteen cents?" Johnny put in quickly.

"OK," his father smiled. "I guess that will be all right."

"Can I do it every day?" Johnny asked.

"No, Johnny, I think that's too much," his father said. "You don't want to take all the work away from Sam. He's shined my shoes for a long time. It wouldn't be fair. I'll give you a pair to do once a week."

Johnny agreed. Fifteen cents a week. Here was another small source of money.

* * * * *

SAVING and earning as Johnny did, he had quite a lot of money in four weeks. He began to think more hopefully about the horse. When he bought the flats of fine plants for the Rolfs, they surely wouldn't be angry at him any more. They might even let him pet Red Boy. And maybe after a while, if he was always careful around their farm they might let him ride again. Maybe their dog would trot along. And maybe he could make real pets of some of the calves. They were as pretty as the wild, young deer in pictures.

He began to collect sugar lumps for Red Boy to use, just in case he could go to the Rolfs' again. He could buy sugar, of course, but he needed his money for the flats. His mother gave him some sugar lumps, but he wanted more. He made a game of finding ways to get them.

Suddenly he thought of a good place to get sugar. The drugstore, of course. One afternoon he stopped in at Singer's, the drugstore he always went to. Three boys and a girl he knew were there. He climbed onto the stool next to them and drew a bowl of lump sugar toward him.

"I want a strawberry ice cream soda, please," he said to the counter man. "And do you mind if I take a lump of your sugar?"

The man said, "The sugar's for people who order coffee or tea. It's not for kids to play with."

Johnny put his quarter back in his pocket and started toward the door.

"Hey," one of the boys called out, "what's the matter with you, Johnny?"

Johnny didn't answer. He walked two blocks south and around a corner to the Wales Drug Store. But as he went up to the counter, he saw that they had no lump sugar. Off he went again, to Halleck's Drug Store, a little farther on. As he went in, Ginger and a younger girl were just sliding off their stools.

"Hi," he said.

"Hi. What are you going to have? A sundae?" Ginger asked.

He told her what he liked best as he looked at the counter. Yes, they had lump sugar here.

"We had chocolate sundaes," Ginger told him. The girls stood for a moment more, talking to him. Johnny took Ginger aside and told her that visiting the drugstore was a part of a plan about his secret—the horse. Ginger smiled and quickly took her friend out of the store, so that she wouldn't ask questions. But as the girls went to the street door, Johnny heard the younger girl ask, "What did Johnny mean about the horse and the secret?"

Johnny smiled to himself as he got on a stool. He knew Ginger wouldn't give the secret away.

The lean, gray-haired man behind the counter came over to him. "What'll you have—" he asked as he wiped the counter clean with his damp cloth.

Johnny said, "Strawberry ice cream soda."

While the man was fixing the drink, Johnny said, "Do you mind if I take just one of your lumps of sugar?"

"No," said the man. "Go ahead. But what do you

want it for?"

Johnny liked the looks of this man. "For a horse," he told him.

"For a horse?" the man repeated after him, and his eyes lighted up. "Well, now, that's a good reason for collecting sugar. And I'm friends with anyone who's a friend of a horse."

Johnny told him about Red Boy. The man listened with interest.

"I'll tell you what, young fellow," he said. "Are you coming in once a week, you say? Every time you come in, I'll give you two lumps of sugar."

Halleck's store and Freddie the counterman got all Johnny's business after that.

The days were getting longer and warmer, and school would soon be out. Johnny had six dollars. He was feeling better and better about the Rolfs and Red Boy.

Now he was ready for the next step in his plans—telling his parents. At suppertime he said, "Mom, Dad, something happened at the Rolfs' that Sunday I went there, when we were at Uncle Howard and Aunt Nora Evers'." He was very serious.

"What happened?" his mother asked, immediately looking worried.

His father asked, "Did you break anything? Is that what you're earning money for, son?"

"Yes," Johnny said. "I mean—I guess it's something like that." He told them the whole story of the afternoon at the Rolfs'.

His parents were horrified. Quickly he explained about the money he had been earning, and the flats of young plants he was going to buy for the Rolfs. Would his parents take him to Murch's Garden Store that Mrs. Halloran had told him about? And would they drive him out to the Rolfs' soon afterward so that he could take the plants to them?

"We certainly will," his mother said, "but you should have told us right away. We are here to help you."

"We'll help you all we can," his father agreed.

That settled, Johnny told them about the horse,

dog, cows, calves, and chickens. But especially he told how he felt about Red Boy.

"When can we go to Murch's to look at plants?" he asked. "Can we go this Saturday?"

"Sure," his father said. "We'll go to Murch's then."

A few days after that, two letters came to the McKees from the Everses. One was for Johnny and one for his parents. Johnny's letter was from Emily and Bill. Emily had written:

DEAR JOHNNY,

My mother and father want you to come here and visit us when school is out. We want you to stay for three weeks at least. My parents are writing your parents to ask if they will let you. Please come. Billy and I want you to. Bring a big suitcase full of stuff so you can stay a long time.

Love,

EMILY AND BILL

The letter Johnny's parents had received from Nora and Howard Evers repeated the invitation. The Everses were eager to have Johnny at their place and hoped he could come early in June. If the McKees couldn't drive Johnny out, he could come by train or bus, they suggested. Howard Evers would meet him at the station where both the buses and the trains came in. In that case, the McKees should let them know on which bus or train to expect Johnny.

"Can I go?" Johnny asked in excitement.

"Of course you may." His mother was happy for him.

So was his father. "It'll be a fine vacation for you," he said. "And now we won't have to drive out there just to take the tomatoes and the flower plants to the Rolfs. We'll take them when we drive you to the Everses'."

Johnny couldn't think of anything he'd rather do in all the world than spend three weeks with the Everses. He and Emily and Bill would do so many

44

things. And maybe if he could make friends with the Rolfs again, he could get Aunt Nora to let him take them over there so that they could see Red Boy and the other animals.

Johnny and his parents wrote separate letters, thanking the Everses for the invitation. And Johnny began to get together the things that he wanted to take along. He laid out his Western hat, his belt and chaps, and the rope with which he practiced roping. He brought out his fishing rod too.

But school would not be out for over a week yet, and it would be two weeks before he could go on his vacation trip. His mother complained that his room looked too disorderly, and he had to put some of his things away again.

On Saturday his father drove him to Murch's Garden Store to find out what plants they could get. The man in charge showed them the flats he had.

"I'm afraid you're too late for our tomatoes," he said. "We sold the last of them last week. They'd be too big for us to handle by now."

45

"Do you know anyone else who might have them?" Mr. McKee asked.

"No. We're the only ones who handle them in this town," the man said.

It was a blow to Johnny. He had been so sure the flats would work out. "Now what would he do?" he asked his father in a low and troubled voice.

His father put his hand on his shoulder. "I'm disappointed, too," he said. "But we aren't farmers, Johnny, and we didn't know enough about these things. Why don't you just give the Rolfs the money you earned for them?"

Johnny knew this wouldn't please the Rolfs as much as fine, sturdy, growing tomato plants would. But it was no doubt the only thing left for him to do now.

"I guess I could bring them some flats of flowers, though," he said. "Let's see. What kind of flowers did they have there?"

He didn't know.

"Better just give them the money," Mr. McKee

said. "They'd understand how hard you tried."

He and Johnny went out of the garden store to-gether. Johnny was silent and thoughtful. He was glad he had the money for the Rolfs, anyway.

✿ 3 ✿

THE BIG FLOOD

School had closed, and vacation time was here at last. The day of Johnny's trip drew near, and once more he gathered the things he wanted to take with him. He began to pack his bag, too, putting in cotton pants and sweatshirts. His mother helped. She added all sorts of clothes he would have forgotten to take, such as ironed shirts for Sundays and socks and a sweater.

Johnny was really most interested in packing his box of sugar lumps for the horse and some presents that his mother had bought him for Emily and Bill. There was a doll's trunk for Emily and a little toy airplane for Bill. Most important of all, of course, was the money he had earned for the Rolfs—seven dollars and twenty-five cents now. He put it in his pocket wallet.

The McKees had planned to drive Johnny out to the Everses' farm on the coming Saturday, but one evening Johnny's father came home from the office and said there would have to be a change. A business matter would keep him in town on Saturday. Mrs. McKee often helped him at the office, and this time it was quite important that she be there, also.

"But you can go alone, Johnny," Mr. McKee told his son. "You can take the train or bus to Newton; that's the nearby town. The Everses will meet you."

"Oh, boy!" said Johnny. He liked that. "I've been on buses so often, I'll take the train."

His mother said, "I'll phone Nora and Howard when we know which train you're going on. I think there's one a few minutes after two o'clock in the afternoon."

The telephone call was made that evening. Uncle Howard Evers said that he would have to go to Newton for seed anyway, and the trip to the station to meet Johnny would be no trouble at all.

Johnny petted his cat, Tim even more than usual these last few days, and the cat followed him around as though he knew Johnny was going away. It had rained almost steadily for four days, and Johnny wore his raincoat as he made his farewell calls in the neighborhood. He spent much time in talking about his vacation with other children, especially with Bart and Ginger, who knew his secret. Sometimes, when the rain stopped, he took Tim with him.

On the day of the journey, he was up early. Now and then he put some extra things in his bag or took something out. He looked once more with pride at the presents for Emily and Bill. He took six sugar lumps out of the box he had in the bottom of his suitcase and put them in his pocket. He liked to have them easily at hand.

Whenever he had the suitcase open, Tim jumped into it.

"I guess he thinks he can go with me that way," Johnny told his mother.

The morning was bright and clear, and Johnny was happy. After breakfast Mrs. McKee went to the office with her husband. Johnny played with Tim, and after a while, went out and visited once more with his friends in the neighborhood. Bart and Ginger each gave him another sugar lump to take to Red Boy. Johnny had a really good supply now.

At about twelve Mrs. McKee came home, and she and Johnny had a lunch of sandwiches and cookies and milk. Then Mrs. McKee wrapped a piece of chocolate cake in wax paper and gave it to Johnny to take along for a snack on the train. Right after that Johnny put on his broad-brimmed Western hat and took all his things out to the car.

Clouds were gathering thickly in the sky, and rain threatened as he and his mother drove to the station. Mrs. McKee and the conductor helped

Johnny board the train with his heavy suitcase, his folding fishing pole, and the new animal book his father had given him. The conductor found him a seat, and he slid over to the window. His suitcase and pole were put in the rack above his head.

His mother kissed him good-bye. He watched her go out to the platform and back to their car and waved to her. The clouds grew darker still. Johnny was sorry. He had hoped that the weather would stay bright so that he and Emily and Bill could play outdoors when he got to the farm.

A large woman in a tan linen suit came into the car and sat down beside him. The train began to move out of the station; in a few minutes it had left Warren City far behind. Johnny looked at the quickly changing scenery outside the window—first the houses and stores, then the woods, fields, and meadows. Suddenly the downpour began. The rain washed against the windows so hard that Johnny could not see through them at all.

"That's quite a storm," the woman beside him

said in astonishment.

"It's a cloudburst," the man in the seat behind said to his wife. For Johnny, the big storm added to the excitement of the trip. Watching the rain against the windows, however, he soon grew restless. He was longing to walk up the aisle and see what the other people in the car were like. But the lady next to him had her magazine open in front of her, and she didn't look as though she would like him to push by her. He sat fidgeting for a while, then finally got up and said, "Excuse me."

She frowned, but let him by.

He walked to the front of the car, got himself a drink of water, and came back to his seat. Soon, however, he got up once more and asked the lady to let him out.

"What, again?" she asked.

He felt a little foolish, but he did like to see things. He went up the aisle again and looked into the next car. Worried about his suitcase and fishing pole and hat and book and cake, however, he soon returned to them.

The woman beside him said, "I wish you'd sit still, boy."

He did for a while. Every now and then the conductor called out the name of a station along the way, and the train came to a stop. People got on each time, shaking rain from their clothes and hats.

Johnny unwrapped his chocolate cake and ate it. Then he started to read his book, opening it at the part about chipmunks. But he was afraid he'd miss something that was going on in the car or outside. Every time he looked up, he lost his place. Finally he gave up trying to read. If only the lady beside him didn't mind his stepping past her, he'd go for a walk again.

It was still raining, but not quite so wildly as at first, and after a while it stopped entirely. Blue sky appeared, but far off the clouds were still a deep purple-black.

The conductor came through the train again. This time he called Johnny's station—Newton.

Johnny jammed his Western hat on his head and asked the lady to let him pass. The conductor was at one end of the car, and Johnny asked him to help with his bag.

"Certainly!" the conductor said, and then, "Your mother asked me to, and I hadn't forgotten."

In another minute Johnny was out on the station platform. And there, just a few steps away, stood Uncle Howard Evers, Emily, and Bill. The children had come along to meet him, too.

Johnny was pleased, and his face was one wide smile as he went to them. Emily and Bill were excited over the cloudburst they had driven through. As Mr. Evers picked up Johnny's big suitcase and led the way to his car, they told Johnny about it.

Mr. Evers' car had a small, two-wheeled trailer cart attached to the back. In it lay three large sacks of vegetable seeds, covered with a heavy plastic sheet.

Johnny liked the little trailer, and asked Uncle Howard, "Can we ride in the cart?"

"Well—" Uncle Howard rubbed his chin and looked a little doubtful.

"Please, Daddy," Emily said.

And Bill echoed, "Please, please, Daddy."

Mr. Evers smiled at the children. "Well, I guess it'll be all right." He scratched his head.

"Oh, thanks," said Johnny quickly. "Thanks."

Mr. Evers took the wet plastic off and said, "OK. In you go. But you've got to promise you'll sit still. No getting up, no hopping around, no changing seats."

The children promised. They climbed in and sat flat in the bottom, leaning against the seed bags. Mr. Evers looked them over. Then he left them and got in behind the wheel of the car. In a moment they were rolling along the country road. Everything felt fine out under the open sky. The clouds were breaking up more and more. Sunshine came through here and there and fell in golden splashes over meadows and woods.

They turned into the Mill River road. The trees

arched overhead on both sides. On the right the waters of the river flowed, and on the left a steep slope rose. The branches of the trees met overhead. Big drops of water from their wet leaves splashed on the children, and they laughed and squealed.

Emily told Johnny about an opossum they had seen hereabouts on their way to the station. They began to watch for the creature, hoping to see it again.

The children were riding backwards. Behind the little trailer car, the road looked like a green tunnel to Johnny. It grew narrower and narrower in the distance. Looking down this leafy way, Johnny suddenly noticed that far off something was different about the river and the road. At first he thought it was only a shadow. Then he saw that a wall of water was rolling toward them. Now he could hear the strange, rumbling, rushing sound it made. Emily noticed it at the same time, and both of them yelled frantically to Mr. Evers. He stopped the car instantly, hearing the fear in the children's voices.

"What's the matter, kids?" he asked, looking back at them.

Johnny was out of the trailer in a second. He got small Bill on his back, piggyback. "A flood! It's a flood!" he yelled, and ran up the slope with Bill. Emily was beside him.

Now Mr. Evers saw it for himself and shouted, "Run, kids! Don't wait for me. I'll get the car out."

As the children thrashed through brush, wet grass, and weeds, they screamed to Mr. Evers to hurry.

Behind them the noise of the oncoming flood grew louder. It was a strange and fearful sound. Trees trembled, and their leaves rustled as the flood hit them. Some were uprooted instantly and were swept away on the swollen mass of water. Rocks and stones on the banks tumbled over and over. In a single minute or less, the flood had reached the car. It filled all the wide river bed behind the children and came high over its banks, rising over the road, the low-lying meadows, and the woods. The children had outrun it; only its outer edge licked at their feet. But the touch of the water frightened them, and they ran still faster.

At last on high ground, they were clear of the water. Johnny let small Bill slide down, and they all turned and looked behind them for Mr. Evers. He and the car were nowhere to be seen. Deep, fast, muddy water rolled where they had been driving.

"Daddy! Daddy!" Emily and Bill shouted.

"Uncle Howard!" Johnny called.

All three of them were terribly afraid for him. They ran along the flood's edge, looking for him. And they called him again and again.

Suddenly, in a clear spot between the trees on the opposite shore, Emily saw her father, looking about him. He had not yet seen them and did not know where they were.

He had jumped from the car a moment too late and had been swept away, but the current and his own good swimming strokes had carried him ashore on the other side.

The children shouted again, and at last the sound of their voices reached him across the ever-widening waters. He threw his arms up in joy, then quickly waved to them to leave the water's edge—to get farther away from danger.

Behind the children, t|

The children, happy that he was safe, climbed to higher ground. Looking back from there, they could see him walking away from the river. But, apparently in worry, he turned at every few steps to watch them. Before long the children had lost sight of him beyond the trees.

...oise of the flood was loud

"What is Daddy going to do?" Emily was almost in tears. "I wish he wouldn't leave us."

At the words "leave us," small Bill began to cry. He was already badly frightened, and this was the last straw. Johnny put an arm over the little boy's shoulders, and he and Emily tried to soothe him.

"He'll be back for us. You know that," Emily said. "Just wait and see."

"Maybe he can't ever get to us over all the water." Bill sobbed. "Where's our car?"

"It's probably lost in the flood," Johnny said. "He'll get another car and come for us."

"He can't get to us in a car," Emily said miserably. "And he hasn't got a boat."

"Maybe he'll get a boat," Johnny suggested.

He looked at the floodwater as it ran by. It was a strong, swift current. Trees and parts of barns and sheds were bobbing along on it. It was much too fast for a boat to cross, he thought. Uncle Howard would have to come from the other side of the hill.

Johnny said, "My suitcase is down there in the

car, under the water. And my sugar, and my fishing pole, and all my things—and your father's
seeds." He didn't mind too much, though. At least
Emily and Bill were out of the water, he told himself.

Johnny and Emily kept Bill between them as
they hurried on, and soon he quieted down. Small
wild animals were running uphill with the children. They, too, were fleeing from the flood. Their
homes and nests and secret hiding places in the
river valley were all under water. There were rabbits and field mice and a strange-looking creature,
a porcupine, but the children could not stop to
enjoy them now.

They looked ahead of them. Just beyond the
top of the long slope they could see the roofs of a
house and barn and the top of a silo.

Emily suddenly cried out, "Look! We're at the
Rolfs' farm." She felt greatly comforted. It was
good to be so near home, even though the flood cut
her off from it.

As Johnny looked about him, he, too, recognized the Rolfs' place. "Gosh," he said.

Faintly he heard the whinnying of the horse, the frightened lowing of cattle, and the chattering of chickens beyond the hill, but he paid little attention to them. He was thinking about the Rolfs, whom he would see in a few minutes. He felt for his wallet in his pocket; the money he had earned was there. He hoped that the Rolfs weren't angry with him anymore, and that they would let him pay for the damage he had caused. If only he could have straightened his problem out with them before having to ask for their help. He and Bill and Emily were going to need their help till the Everses could come, he knew.

He heard the barking of the Rolfs' big, half-collie dog, and called to him, "Here, fellow; here, fellow."

"His name is Shep," Emily explained, and she and Bill called the dog, too.

"Sure, I know his name," Johnny said.

Shep went on barking, but as the children came

nearer and he saw who they were, he ran to them, wagging his tail. They could see that he was still nervous. Even after they petted him, he barked as though he was trying to tell them something.

The children reached the yard of the house. Why were the cattle and the horse making so much noise? The cows and calves were surely safe over there on the other side of the hill, yet something was clearly wrong. Where were the Rolfs? Why weren't they out trying to quiet their farm animals?

Johnny felt that he must find out what troubled the cows. But first he and Emily and Bill should go to the house and see the Rolfs. The back door was closed, and the children knocked. There was no answer. They called, but still no one answered. The Rolfs must be away. Emily tried the door and found that it was not locked. But none of the three children liked to go in uninvited. They stood on the porch, wondering what to do next.

Finally Johnny said, "Emily, will you and Bill

stay here while I go see what's the matter with the cows?"

"Sure," Emily said. "You go and see. They're probably just nervous, though."

The two younger children sat down on the back porch. Two gray cats came to them from the yard, shaking water from their paws, and the children took them in their laps.

Johnny and Shep went off toward the pasture. The dog stopped barking.

✿ 4 ✿

ALL THE ANIMALS

Splashing hurriedly along the wet path, Johnny passed the flower border and saw, to his surprise, that it was full of growing plants. And in the kitchen garden, fine, big tomato plants stood in two neat rows. All of them were much taller than the ones the cows had trampled earlier that year.

"Flats," he said to himself. "The Rolfs must have bought flats."

They must have done it right away and planted them weeks ago. That was the only way that the plants could be as large as they were now, he thought. He felt tremendously glad that everything was in such fine shape. But he could not stop to look further. The bellowing of the cattle and Red Boy's sharp, frightened whinnying kept him going up the slight rise beyond the house toward the valley pastures that lay on the other side of the farm road.

"Red Boy! Red Boy, I'm here!" he shouted. And, "OK, you cows and calves. OK!"

In a moment he came over the top of the rise, and there he saw what had frightened the horse and cows. The pasture on their side of the hill was flooded, also. A great lake lay all about the animals. Except for a few close to the fence, they were already standing knee-deep in water. All who could were pushing against the fence near the gate, trying to get out and away from the danger. But they could not.

"Why was the floodwater over here, too?" Johnny wondered. Then he remembered that the river made a horseshoe curve that looped around the dairy farm. He turned south and north. The flooded river had poured its water into the whole valley on every side and had reached all around the Rolfs' hill. The few acres on which the house and barn stood had become an island. He and Emily and Bill and all the animals were cut off from the rest of the world.

He felt awed and afraid. But he pulled himself together. The horse and the cattle must be let out of their pasture, he knew. If the water rose even a little more, they would drown. He must let them out quickly and bring them to the higher ground around the house. He felt some fear of the cattle because they were so big and so nervous. But, after all, he could stay behind the gate and so protect himself.

Johnny's hand reached to open the gate. Then he stopped, horrified at the thought of what would happen to the flowers, the lawn, and probably the tomatoes.

What had happened the last time he was there would happen all over again. Only this time it would be a hundred times worse. This time thirty or more cows and calves would trample the lawn, instead of a few. And they would trample it even worse because they were so frightened.

And would the frail wire fence around the little vegetable garden hold when the herd of big animals milled around it? It was not very likely. Johnny could imagine how all those fine, tall, new tomato plants would look, crushed under the hoofs of this herd.

He put his hands over his face. He could not bear to make this terrible thing happen—and by opening the gate he would. And the Rolfs—they would be angrier at him than ever. Oh, no, he could not ruin the Rolfs' place again.

But if he didn't, Red Boy and the cattle would drown. He couldn't stand by and let them die.

He said to himself, "Aren't the cattle and horse really more important than the lawn or this little garden?"

Shep was barking again, barking hard as though

he was begging Johnny to do something to save the farm animals. Johnny closed his mind to any further sorrow about the vegetables and flowers. He opened the big gate, keeping behind it.

Instantly the cows pushed through. They pressed against the gate, swinging it wide. Shep stood aside, barking. But now he sounded pleased and as though he was urging them to trot out faster.

Here came the horse.

"Hey, Red Boy," Johnny called, his voice warm with his love for the animal.

Johnny climbed to the top of the gate and straddled it, his legs hugging tightly against it. He reached out his hand and tried to touch the horse as he passed. Red Boy saw him but was too far away and too much in a hurry to stop for Johnny. He trotted by, raising his head and shaking it, impatient with the cattle in front of him.

Johnny glanced toward the house and saw that Emily and Bill had come out over the rise to see what he was doing. They were cheering for him.

71

He yelled to them to go back.

"This big herd will trample you," he said.

They took one look at the oncoming cattle and ran to the porch again as fast as they could. Both of them shrieked with excitement.

Johnny turned back to his work. Now he must get the calves, and they could be reached only through the cow pasture. He and the dog made their way toward them, keeping close to the upper fence. This part of the pasture was still above the flood, yet they were walking at the edge of the sea of water. Johnny looked at the fence posts. He noticed how deep they stood in the water. Later it would be easy to tell by them whether the flood was still rising.

He looked across the water, on which trees and broken branches continued to sweep by. He hoped for a glimpse of people or houses beyond the flood, but all he could see was the thick strip of woods along the river. It was like a screen, cutting off all view of the houses or roads that might be beyond it.

"Hey, Red Boy," Johnny called at the horse

The calves were crying, and Johnny started to run, splashing heavily as he went. In a moment he had reached them. He let them out quickly and with Shep, who was so good at herding, drove them along the upper fence. He and the dog had trouble with them, however, because the calves did not like the water. Afraid and confused, they sometimes stood still or tried to go back to their own pasture. But at last Johnny and Shep drove them through the gate and into the yard.

"Good dog," Johnny said when he had closed the

73

gate behind them. "You're smart, Shep, and a real pal."

In the yard the cows found their young and the calves their mothers. The calves suckled as their mothers licked them with great wet tongues.

Shep stopped barking. The cattle were where he wanted them. He felt free to do as he liked and dashed off to chase three half-grown rabbits that sat nearby. But Johnny stopped him.

"Come back here, Shep," he said. "Those rabbits can't get back to their woods. The woods are under water. Shep! Leave them alone. Here, Shep."

The dog was surprised at such an order. He had always been allowed to chase rabbits, but he was willing to obey Johnny.

"We're going to rescue the chickens now," Johnny told Shep, putting his hand on his head. But to get over to the chicken pen beside the barn, Johnny had to walk through the milling herd of cattle. He felt small and light, knowing how easily the nervous creatures could trample and crush him.

He looked around for Red Boy. There he was, not more than twenty feet away. Johnny pulled a lump of sugar from his pocket and held it out to the horse. Red Boy came to him this time. As Johnny gave him the sugar lump, he put one arm on Red Boy's neck and laid his cheek against him.

For weeks he had longed for the horse, and he was hugging him at last. But he could not stand still for long. Holding on to Red Boy's dark mane, Johnny pushed against him, and they started to walk toward the chicken pen. He was using the horse as a shield between himself and the cattle.

"Johnny! Wait!" It was Emily calling from close behind him. He turned, and there she was, a few feet away.

Johnny was surprised. "Emily! You shouldn't have come," he cried. "The cattle will trample and kill you. They're so scared."

"I'm all right. I came way around the other side of the cows and along the fence," she said. She had a basket in one hand and a dishpan in the other.

"But why did you have to come?" Johnny asked impatiently. "I'll take care of the chickens. Will Bill be OK alone up there at the house? He won't come out here too?"

"No. He's OK," Emily said. "He's scared of cows. He'll stay at the house. And I like the chickens. I want to help save them, the way you did the cows."

"What are the dishpan and basket for?" Johnny asked.

Emily said, "They're for mother hens with little chicks. I brought these to carry them in if there are any."

"Oh." Johnny was surprised and pleased that she had thought of this. She was a great help after all.

It took but a few minutes to let the hens out of their pen. And there was only one mother hen with very young chicks. She tried to peck the children. But Emily held the hen's head back with a piece of board while Johnny got her chicks out. She hopped into the basket after them fast enough.

76

After that, Johnny stopped at the barn for the horse's bridle. The floodwater was lapping the back wall of the barn, and a little of it was leaking in. Johnny shuddered as he looked at it. But he needed the bridle. He ran to it, snatched it off its hook, and was outdoors again in less than a minute. With this, he and Emily and Bill could ride Red Boy when they needed to. Riding would be important to them, with the big, restless cattle all over the place. He put the bridle on the horse at once. But he and Emily were unable to ride because they had the basket to carry. Again they used Red Boy to shield themselves as they made their way to the house. The cows moved out of the way as the horse walked along and as Johnny shouted at them.

On the back porch Bill greeted them in excitement. "One of the cats caught a squirrel," he told them. "I put both cats indoors. Don't let them out."

"Of course we won't," Johnny said. "You did exactly the right thing."

He felt very strongly that the little animals who

had run away from the flood must be protected.
They had the same right to be saved as he and Bill
and Emily had. No cat or dog should eat any of the
wild ones.

Emily said, "We have to take the mother hen
indoors. It's safer for her and her babies there. The
raccoons or opossums might get her babies outdoors."

The children went in, though they felt shy about
doing it. They set the basket down on the kitchen
floor and watched the mother hen and her chicks
for a while.

Then Emily ran to look for a telephone. "I'm going to call Mom," she said.

The telephone was in the front hall, but when
Emily picked it up there was no sound. She was
disappointed.

Johnny, who had followed her, said, "The lines
must be down because of the flood." He tried the
light switch. The electricity was off, too.

"Let's go outside again," he said to Emily, who

was still trying to telephone. "I don't like to be in here, with the Rolfs not home."

Emily put the phone down, and they went to the porch once more. Bill, who had been playing with the cats, left them and came too. All three sat on the top step, feeling lonely and looking at all their animals.

But Johnny was worried and could not keep still for long. What if the flood should rise over their whole island? He would not tell Emily and Bill his thought, but he knew that if this happened, he and Bill and Emily, and all the animals around them, would drown. He *must* go and see how bad the danger was.

He would ride the horse, and he would take Emily and Bill with him, for he felt more comfortable when all three were close together. Red Boy's back was broad—strong enough for them all.

Bill and Emily were eager to go with Johnny, but first they put Shep indoors so that he could not chase rabbits. Johnny had tied Red Boy to the porch rail by his bridle. Now all three of the children climbed onto his back from the railing. The plan worked fine. Johnny sat in front and held the reins. Bill came next, and Emily sat behind him so that she could hold him if he slipped. They set out to ride slowly about the place.

First of all, Johnny took the horse around the northwest side of the house toward the pastures where the cows and calves had been. There he took a quick, secret look at the fence and posts he had watched before. They were under water now. If he had left the horse and cattle there, they would have died. He was glad they were alive and trampling the ground around the house.

"Flood, please don't come farther up," Johnny said to himself. And he made a little prayer to God to please keep him and his friends safe, together with his animals, tame and wild. But still he said nothing to the other two children about the danger he feared.

He took the horse around toward the flower

border and the kitchen garden. Though he could hardly bear to look, sooner or later he must know what the cattle had done to the plants. A quick glance made him catch his breath.

The flower border had already gone under the hoofs of the animals. It was a sickening sight. The vegetable garden was still all right, but the light, surrounding fence was beginning to lean over as the cows pushed against it. One cow stretched her neck out over a broken part, reaching for a juicy green bite. The garden too would soon be trampled. Johnny could imagine the Rolfs' faces when they saw it.

He shouted to the cows to go away. He hurried Red Boy to the fence and slapped at them. A dozen other cows stood nearby. They too were pushing against the fence. Suddenly it fell over, and in they went.

"Shoo!" Johnny cried. "Shoo!" But the cows did not pay any attention to him.

Emily and Bill had not known what had

"Shoo!" Johnny cried at the cows. "Shoo!"

happened to the Rolfs' garden in the spring. Now he told them and went on to explain how he had worked for weeks to earn money to repay the Rolfs.

The younger children understood what a misfortune it was for Johnny that the garden was ruined again.

Emily said, "There are too many cows though, Johnny. We can't stop them."

"I know," Johnny said, and he felt tears in his eyes.

"Let's go away from here," Bill said.

"Yes," Emily urged. "Don't let's look at them trampling the garden. It just makes us feel terrible."

Johnny agreed, but he was not comforted. His heart was heavy as he turned Red Boy away.

The three rode on and soon were out from among the rest of the cows. They rode toward the spot where they had come up from the river road only a short time ago. Johnny held Red Boy's reins slack, and the horse walked slowly. Nevertheless his big hoofs startled little animals who were hiding in the weeds and bushes along his path. A muskrat, some chipmunks, and some squirrels scattered before him. Four or five rabbits hopped away. A garden snake slithered gracefully through the grass. How very many animals there were! Animals everywhere!

The children came to another slight rise in the ground, and again Johnny could see the whole wide stretch of the floodwaters that made an island of the small piece of land on which they were. And the island was the shape of a ship.

"Emily, Bill, look," Johnny cried. "We're on an island that's like an ark. We're like Noah and his family. We brought the cows and calves and horse and chickens on our ark. And these wild animals have come up here, too, to be saved."

"Yes." Emily was thrilled. "We're on an island ark. It really is like Noah's Ark in the Bible, Johnny." But then her face grew sober. "Do you think we'll be on this island ark for weeks and weeks, or maybe even for forty days and forty nights, like Noah?"

"No," said young Bill. "We'll make ourselves a boat and go home."

"Maybe we will." Emily's lips trembled. "We can't stay here forever."

Johnny said, "I really think someone will come in a boat if the flood lasts very long." He stopped, and cried, "Look!" as he pointed to a tree. Two raccoons and their four young, handsome in their brown-black and white fur, were climbing into it.

Bill and Emily squealed with excitement. For a moment their worries were forgotten in the pleasure of seeing these wild creatures.

The mother raccoon heard them, then saw them and instantly dropped from her branch and ran off.

Johnny chuckled. "She's trying to make us chase her," he said, "so we'll leave her children alone." He had read that the mothers of young raccoons did that.

"Let's go away," Emily said. "We don't want to scare her."

Johnny made Red Boy go a little faster. Then they saw the deer. There were three of them, and they were standing behind a clump of bushes to the south. The youngest one was nibbling green shoots, and the other two stood alert, their heads and graceful ears up, their dark eyes wide. One was a buck, Johnny knew, because he had started to grow antlers. The three deer were a family, that was clear—father, mother, and their young one. The buck stood forward with the doe and the young one a little behind him as though he was protecting them.

The two bigger deer stood alert, their heads up

Johnny had never before seen live deer, and he was beside himself with joy. He could see that Emily and Bill were, too. They made little whispering, murmuring sounds, telling each other how wonderful this sight was.

Sitting very still, the children watched for quite a while. But the deer knew that they were there and were nervous. There was no place for them to run. This was such a little place, this island ark of dry land. And it was so full of other animals, walking, stalking, mooing, creeping, hopping.

"We'd better go on," Emily whispered. "We don't want to scare them too much."

Johnny roused himself and nodded. "No, we don't want to scare them," he agreed. And they rode on, hard though it was to leave the deer.

In a moment they saw an opossum, clumsy and heavy, trundling through the low grass. It, too, looked as though it wanted to find shelter.

Two field mice sat on a stone. One was wiping its whiskers with its tiny paws. The other seemed to be looking directly at the three children on the horse. Its eyes were bright and round. The little animals scampered away as the horse's hoofs came near them.

Farther on, a skunk showed itself for a moment then went off among some weeds. In a moment a fox came into view. Restless and nervous, he was slipping along the water's edge, wanting badly to escape from the island. One of the chickens that Johnny and Emily had let out of the pen was scratching nearby, and the fox eyed it. But he did not try to catch it; he was badly frightened out here in the open.

In the trees and on the roof of the house there were many birds. Some hopped about. Some flew here and there. Most were silent, but a few of them, like the big blue jays and the crows, were making sharp noises of alarm.

A red-winged blackbird flew so near the children on the horse that they could feel the fanning of his wings. A catbird on a branch cocked his head. His bright, round eyes met Johnny's. He seemed to be asking why this strange and fearful flood had happened. Forgetting all the notes and sounds he could make, the bird sat twitching his tail and turning his head.

A hawk rose from a log and seemed to leap into the air. He landed high on a treetop and looked about him.

Johnny stopped the horse, and the children sat watching the creatures and talking softly to each other.

Johnny felt tremendously happy. He thought to himself how strange it was that he could be so happy with all the danger about him, and all the worries . . . and with his sugar lumps lost in the car along with his bag and Emily's and Bill's presents and all the other things. Still, there could be nothing more wonderful than to be on the horse and among the animals. He had never even hoped to be so close to so many of them in the air, on the ground, and in the trees.

The voices of Emily and Bill roused him from his thoughts.

"Our bridge is under the water," Emily said in awe.

"Where is our house?" Bill asked.

Emily pointed. "Over there."

"I can't see it," Bill said.

"Of course you can't," Emily said. "The trees hide it from us."

"I *want* to see it. I want to go home," the little boy said. "I want to see Mom and Daddy."

Emily didn't answer.

Johnny began to think of his own parents. "I wonder what our mothers and fathers are doing right now," he said.

He was thinking that perhaps his parents, far off in Warren City, knew nothing about all that had happened to him on this remarkable afternoon. But still, the telephone lines out there beyond the flood might be all right. If so, Uncle Howard Evers had surely called Johnny's mother and father and told them. They would be worried.

The thought made him uneasy. He slapped Red Boy's reins, and the horse walked on.

At last the three came to the place where they had run up from the river about two hours ago. Here, too, the young trees and low bushes that had been well above the flood at that time stood deep in water. But Johnny could see that the current was moving more slowly. The broken branches

90

it carried were not rushing by quite so fast. And, best sign of all, wet branches and leaves lay on the bank. It was clear that they had been left there by retreating water.

Johnny made a little prayer of thanks. Everyone was going to be safe here after all. He was glad that he hadn't told Emily and Bill of his fear that the flood might cover all the hill.

🌿 5 🌿

WITH MANY THANKS

Evening was coming on. The sun dipped behind the clouds that stood over the horizon and touched their edges with fiery color. Before long it would set. The children began to wonder what they should do if no one rescued them that night.

Emily was frowning. "It's getting late," she said. "Let's go back to the house."

"Yes, I want to go to the house," Bill said.

"OK." Johnny slapped the reins again, and Red Boy moved forward quickly.

Once more the children rode through the herd of cows and calves. The animals were bellowing more loudly.

Emily said, "It's because they're used to being milked and fed grain mash this time in the evening."

They slid off Red Boy and onto the porch. Johnny brushed the bangs on Red Boy's forehead and rubbed his nose. The horse nickered softly.

"We can go inside the house and stay," Emily said. "The Rolfs are friends of my parents."

"But maybe they won't like it, anyway," Johnny said. After all, the Rolfs certainly didn't think of him as a friend, he was sure.

He decided, however, that they should risk going in. After all, they might even have to sleep there. They couldn't sleep outdoors all night. That seemed certain.

They went into the kitchen, and Johnny pressed the light switch again to see if the electricity might have come on. Of course it hadn't.

"Well, we don't really need lights yet, I guess," he said.

But Emily was thinking ahead. "We'd better look for candles," she said, "so that we'll have them ready when it gets really dark and we need them."

The boys agreed and began to hunt for them. Emily found some in the kitchen cabinet and put them on the table, together with a box of matches. Then the three decided to look around the house just a little more; they still felt strange in it without the Rolfs.

In the living room they found a television set and in the bedroom a radio. If only they could turn these on, they wouldn't feel so out of touch with the rest of the world, and maybe they could get some news about what was going on in the nearby houses and towns. But radio and television were dead, too, without electricity.

"I'm hungry," Bill said.

Suddenly the other two knew that they were, too—very, very hungry. It was long past their usual suppertime and well past Bill's bedtime.

"Do you think the Rolfs would mind if we ate

some of their food?" Emily asked the boys. "I'm starving, and I want some."

Johnny shook his head. "I don't think we should take anything," he said. He was in trouble enough with the Rolfs, without adding to it, he thought. Still, he was very hungry.

Bill opened the refrigerator, and Johnny and Emily pressed forward to look in. A big, pink boiled ham wrapped in wax paper sat on the shelf with peanut butter, American cheese, butter, and milk near it. How good it all looked.

"I don't think Mr. and Mrs. Rolf would mind our taking some," Emily said. "They wouldn't want us to be hungry."

"I'm hungry," Bill said again.

"Anyway, our parents will pay them back for what we eat. I know they will," Emily said.

Johnny was getting hungrier and hungrier as he looked at the food. Now he said, "Let's eat a *little*, anyway."

They took milk, peanut butter, cheese, and butter out and set them on the kitchen table. After a little searching they found bread in a box on a cabinet. They made sandwiches and ate them eagerly and drank all the milk they wanted. After all, the Rolfs had a herd of cows; there was no need to feel shy about taking the milk, anyway.

Shep sat beside the table, and his eyes followed every motion the children made.

"We forgot Shep," Johnny said. "He's hungry, too."

He stopped eating long enough to find a can of dog food in the pantry and gave Shep some of it.

Billy crumbled up some soft bread for the mother hen and her small chicks.

The two cats came from the living room, crying, "*Meow, meow.*" Emily set a bowl of milk on the floor for them.

Outside there were suddenly squeaks and squeals. Maybe the wild creatures were getting hungry, too, and some were trying to catch others for their supper. Johnny wished he could protect them all—the rabbits and chipmunks from the fox, the chickens from the opossum, the small birds and field mice from the hawk.

All the while the cows were bellowing. The noise they made filled the house and rang out over the wet woods and meadows.

"The poor cows," Johnny said. "I wish we could take care of them the way Mr. Rolf does. But we couldn't milk even one. And there are about thirty of them. I don't even know how we could ever get enough hay for them all from the barn."

The sad mooing made the children feel lonely, and with dusk beginning to fall, the feeling grew deeper. They wished the telephone wasn't out of order. They wished they could look at television.

When they had finished their supper, Johnny, Bill, and Emily went out to the front porch and then to the back porch. They looked across the floodwater in hope that someone might be coming for them in a boat. There was no one anywhere to be seen in all the lonely miles of watery countryside.

97

Bill was growing more and more tired. "I want to go home," he said and started to cry.

Emily and Johnny tried to comfort him. Finally Emily took him into the house and put him on a bed. She started to tell him a story as her mother often did at bedtime. "Maybe he will fall asleep," she thought.

Johnny, with Shep at his side, stayed out on the porch, wishing to be with the animals of his island ark as long as he could. He talked to Red Boy. The horse bobbed his head as if in answer, and once, he snorted. The cattle had moved away from the house a little, and there was a small clear space on the lawn by the porch. Johnny untied the horse and went down and held the rein while Red Boy grazed a little.

The sun was dropping below the horizon. Its upper edge, a golden curve, could still be seen. Johnny climbed on the railing. From there he could see the water and knew that it was still going down. The fence posts stood out well above it now.

Happily he patted Red Boy, who was so friendly and so quiet. Johnny wondered how he would ever get along without Red Boy when he left here, after the flood was over. He gave the horse the last piece of sugar from his pocket.

Shep, still disturbed by the many wild animals in the yard, growled softly now and then. Johnny, his hand on the dog's collar, pushed him through the door of the house and closed it quickly behind him.

The clouds in the blue sky became rosy and lavender and gold. A beautiful sunset painted the sky. A chipmunk, coming out from under the house, sat up on his hind legs and looked at Johnny, quite unafraid. Johnny wondered whether the animal's family had been saved from the flood. He hoped so. He thought of the whole creeping, stirring, flitting, resting lot of animals on the island ark. "How many of them were there?" he wondered. With the deer, the opossum, all the squirrels and chipmunks, the rabbits, the field mice and raccoons, as well as the chickens, the cattle, the horse, the dog, the cats, and the many birds, there must be more than a hundred animals, maybe even two hundred, he thought.

He put his head against Red Boy and went back over the happenings of this remarkable afternoon, thinking about them hard, so that he would never forget them all the rest of his life. Red Boy turned his head and nuzzled him.

Suddenly there was a shout from away off, "Hello. Hello there."

Johnny looked to the east. In the rosy light he saw a rowboat coming across the water. In it were two men.

Johnny shouted and waved to the men, then called to Emily and Bill. They came running.

"Hello," one of the men called again as the boat drew nearer. "Are you children all right?" It sounded like Mr. Evers.

The three children answered all at the same time. "Yes, we're all right," they said, and, "Sure!" and, "We're OK."

"Is that really you, Daddy?" Emily shouted.

"Daddy! Daddy!" Bill cried. He was wide awake now.

"Yes, it's me," Mr. Evers called back, cupping his hands around his mouth. "And Mr. Rolf's with me."

Johnny was afraid of Mr. Rolf. He wished he need not face him. But he must. He climbed onto Red Boy's back.

"Let's go see them," he said to Emily and Bill.

Emily lifted Bill up, and Johnny pulled him from above. Then Emily climbed onto the horse. They made their way toward the place where the boat was pulling to the shore.

Johnny thought to himself, "Now I'll hear Mr. Rolf get good and mad because his garden and lawn and flowers are ruined again. And I'm the one who did it." He braced himself.

By the time the children reached the water's edge, the two men were getting out of the boat. They came striding quickly toward Red Boy and the children.

Mr. Evers reached up and hugged his two children and Johnny.

"I give thanks to God you're safe," he said.

"We were afraid maybe *you* weren't safe," Emily told him.

"I had a good scare," Mr. Evers said. "But I got out of the river all right, as you saw. I guess we lost our car, though. It's somewhere down under that water."

"Are you children all right?"

Mr. Rolf had been looking around him in the summer dusk, and now he asked in a strange voice, "Who let the cattle out?"

Johnny wanted to answer, but for a moment he couldn't. Emily answered for him. "Johnny did," she said proudly. "He did it all by himself. Bill and I stayed on the porch."

Mr. Evers shouted

Johnny said, "I'm sorry about the flowers and the tomato plants. I—"

Mr. Rolf said joyfully, "You saved my cattle. Son, you saved my cattle."

"But the garden—" Johnny said again.

"The garden?" Mr. Rolf looked at him. "Don't let that worry you. We make our living by our dairy cattle, boy, not by our few tomatoes and carrots and flowers."

It was all right, after all. Johnny smiled, feeling better. He slid off the horse quickly and took from his pocket the money he had saved. He held it out to Mr. Rolf.

"This is for the plants I ruined this spring," he said.

Mr. Rolf stared at him, puzzled. "What's this?" he asked. "You want to give me money?"

"I earned it especially so that I could pay for your plants that were spoiled," Johnny went on.

Mr. Rolf pushed the boy's hand away gently but firmly. "Put that back in your pocket," he said.

"You don't owe me anything." He smiled at Johnny, and added, "But I owe you a lot."

Johnny stood staring at Mr. Rolf, uncertain as to what he should do with the money.

Mr. Rolf rubbed his chin. He seemed to be thinking something over. He went to the horse and rubbed his neck.

"The boy saved you too, old fellow, along with my cows. You know that?" he said.

Johnny said, "I love Red Boy. I wouldn't have let anything happen to him."

"Well, now, that's fine," said Mr. Rolf. "I wanted to think of something to do for you for saving my cattle, and this settles it. I'll give you the horse."

Johnny drew in his breath so sharply that it sounded almost like a gasp. "Gosh, you wouldn't really?" he cried. "You wouldn't really give me Red Boy?"

"Certainly," Mr. Rolf said. "The horse has missed having a boy around to ride him and to be friends with. I'll be glad to see him go to you."

"Thanks. Oh thanks." Johnny was the happiest person in the United States for one moment. Then he remembered that he couldn't take the horse because he lived in a city apartment. There was no place for a horse, no place at all. He looked first at Mr. Rolf and then at Uncle Howard Evers, and his face grew long and sad.

Uncle Howard knew what Johnny was thinking. "Oh, well. I guess we can make some kind of arrangement," he said, and paused. He scratched his head thoughtfully. Then he went on, "Say! I'll keep Red Boy on our farm for you, Johnny. And you can come out and ride him every summer."

Emily and Bill, on the horse's back, had been wriggling and squirming with delight. Now they squealed and climbed off the horse.

"Sure, Johnny can come every summer," Emily said.

"Every single summer," Bill echoed.

"That's a good plan," Mr. Rolf said to Mr. Evers. "OK. The horse is yours, Johnny."

Johnny said, "Thank you, Mr. Rolf. Thank you, Uncle Howard." What had happened was better than anything he had ever expected in his life.

He was still holding the money in his hand. Now he said, "Uncle Howard, if Mr. Rolf won't take this, maybe you can use it to buy extra feed and things for Red Boy."

"But the horse won't need much extra in food," Mr. Evers said. "Besides, Emily and Bill can look after him for you while you're in town, winters. And I expect they'll be getting some fun out of him, too. So I won't charge for any board or care."

"The horse is yours, Johnny," said Mr. Rolf

"But I want this to be my horse's money," Johnny said. "I want to pay for some of his extras." He held the money out to Uncle Howard.

"I see. Well, that's fine," Mr. Evers said and took it. He put it carefully into his wallet.

The cows had been bellowing loudly all this time. Mr. Rolf gave one of them an affectionate pat. "Now I'd better attend to my cows," he said. He called to Shep and started to walk away.

"But you can't milk them alone—all those thirty cows," Emily said.

"And there isn't any electricity for your milking machines," Johnny told him.

"I know," said Mr. Rolf. "I'm prepared for that. Howard Evers, here, and some more friends and neighbors from the other side of the river are coming to help me. We'll have to do it by hand. Look over there. See? They're coming now."

The children looked as Mr. Rolf pointed. Two more boats, one with three men in it, the other with two, were halfway across the flooded river.

"By morning," Mr. Evers said, "the river will be near normal, and the electric company will get the lines fixed up."

Mr. Rolf began to herd the cows together. "Where's that dog?" he asked. "Hey! Shep!"

"He can't come," Bill said, suddenly remembering. "We've got him shut up in the house."

"I'll go let him out," Mr. Evers said. "He's needed now."

Johnny explained to Mr. Rolf, "We only shut Shep up in there because we didn't want him to eat the little wild animals that are all over the place. They came up here to get away from the flood and were saved, and—" He looked at Mr. Rolf. "Would you please not let the cats or Shep catch them? We'd like them to get back to their hiding places in the river bottom when the water goes down."

Mr. Rolf looked about him. "What all is up here?" he asked.

"Raccoons, and three deer, an opossum," Johnny began, smiling happily, and Bill and Emily named

109

more of the animals they had seen.

"My goodness." Mr. Rolf was astounded, and he said, almost to himself, "A lot of animals always get drowned in a flood. These must have been at the upper edge of it."

In a gentle voice he said to Johnny, "Sure. I'll give the wild creatures a chance to get back to the woods."

Again he patted a cow who came up to him. She started to lick at him with her big, wet tongue.

"Hey, quit that," Mr. Rolf said affectionately.

Suddenly Emily remembered the food that she and Johnny and Bill had eaten. She told Mr. Rolf about it.

"Was it all right?" she asked.

"Certainly," said Mr. Rolf. "I'm very glad you had sense enough to get yourselves a little supper."

Shep came bounding out of the house now and greeted Mr. Rolf loudly. He pranced around him and then around Johnny and barked. It was as though he wanted to explain about the cattle being saved.

The beautiful afterglow of pink and gold and rose was still spread over the sky. The men who were crossing the river had landed. They came quickly and helped Mr. Rolf and Shep herd the cows toward the barn. Mr. Evers and Johnny joined them.

Johnny took this moment to ask if his parents knew about the flood.

"Yes," said Uncle Howard.

Some of the telephone lines on the other side of the river had already been repaired, and he had been able to get a call through.

"We'll phone them again as soon as we get to the service station up the road," he said. "And you can speak to them yourself."

All the cows were soon in their stalls. Johnny helped the men carry buckets full of grain mash to each of them and bring clean buckets and cans from the milk room and the house. He helped gather flashlights too, and lanterns, for it was already dusky in the barn.

The sound of the men talking and the hungry cows eating and snorting filled the barn with pleasant sound. The men had begun to milk. When the buckets were full, they emptied them into the big cans Mr. Rolf always used and went back to milking again.

Emily and Bill had come to the barn and stood watching with Johnny. The children's faces were bright and full of the excitement of the day.

Well before darkness finally came, Mr. Evers stopped milking to take the children across the water. Driftwood still floated by, and rowing in pitch-darkness would be dangerous.

Mr. Rolf shook Johnny's hand when he said good-bye. "Come for your horse tomorrow or whenever the river's down enough to make the bridge safe for crossing," he said.

"Sure," Johnny said. "I sure will."

"And come to see us often. Mrs. Rolf will be glad to see you, too," Mr. Rolf went on.

Johnny went to Red Boy and patted him once

more. Then he and Mr. Evers, with Emily and Bill, went to the floodwater's edge and got into one of the boats. As Mr. Evers rowed across, he stopped once to keep the boat from being caught by the branches of an uprooted tree that floated by. And once, the boat passed close to some floating planks that had been part of a barn or shed.

Johnny looked back to the island ark. It spread quiet and peaceful in the late dusk of the summer day. He could faintly see the alert, watchful deer behind the bushes to the south. And though he could not see the smaller wild animals, he knew they were there. A few chickens still strutted around. The others were already roosting in a tree. Red Boy was grazing on the lawn.

The flood had brought danger and loss, Johnny thought, but how much had happened that was wonderful, too.

He knew he would always have a very special feeling for the Rolfs and their farm on this hill that had been an island ark today. They and their place and their farm animals seemed, in some way, to belong to him a little now. And the wild animals— he would never lose these creatures who had shared the hill with him and his two friends. They would be all around him whenever he walked in these woods, or whenever he and Red Boy crossed the valley pastures. They would be back in the green and leafy places that hid them so well and that were their homes.

More Books from The Good and the Beautiful Library

Mammals of Small Pond
By Phoebe Erickson

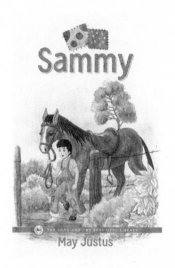

Sammy
By May Justus

Pumpkin, Ginger, and Spice
By Margaret Otto

Calico
By Ethel Calvert Phillips

goodandbeautiful.com